PREVENTION MAGAZINE'S
QUICK & HEALTHY LOW-FAT COOKING

Fabulous
No-Guilt Desserts

From sorbet to chocolate cake,
sin-free desserts for every occasion

❧ ❧ ❧

Rodale Press, Inc.
Emmaus, Pennsylvania

QUICK AND HEALTHY LOW-FAT COOKING

Managing Editor: JEAN ROGERS
Executive Editor: DEBORA T. YOST
Senior Book Designer: DARLENE SCHNECK
Art Director: JANE COLBY KNUTILA
Associate Art Director: ELIZABETH OTWELL

Fabulous No-Guilt Desserts was produced by Rebus, Inc.
Editor: MARYA DALRYMPLE
Recipe Development: MIRIAM RUBIN, JANE YAGODA GOODMAN,
    MARIANNE ZANZARELLA
Writer: BONNIE J. SLOTNICK
Art Director and Designer: JUDITH HENRY
Production Editor: MICHELE HEARNS

Photographer: ANGELO CAGGIANO
Food Stylist: DIANE SIMONE VEZZA
Prop Stylist: VALORIE FISHER
Nutritional Analyses: HILL NUTRITION ASSOCIATES

Copyright © 1996 by Rodale Press, Inc.
Photographs copyright © 1996 by Angelo Caggiano
Front Cover: Devil's Food Cake with Raspberries (recipe on page 110)

Prevention is a registered trademark of Rodale Press, Inc.
Printed in the United States of America on acid-free ⊗, recycled paper ♻

Library of Congress Cataloging-in-Publication Data

Fabulous no-guilt desserts: from sorbet to chocolate cake, sin-free desserts
    for every occasion.
    p.   cm. — (Prevention magazine's quick & healthy low-fat cooking)
    Includes index.
    ISBN 0–87596–328–5   hardcover
    ISBN 0–87596–329–3   paperback
    1. Desserts.   2. Low-fat diet—Recipes.   I. Series
TX773.F23   1996
641.8'6—dc20   96–7287

Distributed in the book trade by St. Martin's Press

2   4   6   8   10   9   7   5   3   1   hardcover
2   4   6   8   10   9   7   5   3   1   paperback

CONTENTS

⅌ ⅌ ⅌

OTHER BOOKS IN THE QUICK & HEALTHY
LOW-FAT COOKING SERIES

Pastas and Sauces
Healthy Home Cooking
Light Ways with Poultry
Easy One-Dish Meals
Healthy Italian Cooking

OTHER RECENT COOKBOOKS FROM RODALE PRESS

Jacques Pépin's Simple and Healthy Cooking
Prevention's Healthy One-Dish Meals in Minutes
Healthy Favorites from America's Community Cookbooks
Evelyn Tribole's Healthy Homestyle Cooking
Healthy Cooking for Two (or Just You)
New Vegetarian Cuisine
100% Pleasure: The Low-Fat Cookbook for People Who Love to Eat
Your Family Will Love It!
Prevention's Stop Dieting and Lose Weight Cookbook
Prevention's Cooking for Good Health

To obtain more information about any of the Rodale Press
cookbooks listed above, please call 1-800-848-4735.

PREFACE

✢ ✢ ✢

Do you feel a little guilty indulging in desserts—even low-fat ones like those in this book? Perhaps your conscience would rest easier if those delicious sweets came on the heels of a really nutritious meal.

We asked a panel of nutrition experts to suggest the perfect menu. Here's what they said: Start with a super salad. Greens are a treasure trove of substances that help protect against cancer, circulatory diseases and many problems linked to aging. With lots of vitamins and minerals, no fat and few calories, greens are true superfoods. Toss up a mixture of romaine, collards, arugula, mâche and other crisp, colorful leaves.

But don't stop there. Throw in a good handful of chick-peas or cubes of tofu for their fiber, B vitamins and cancer-preventing phyto-estrogens. Dress your salad with a heart-smart mixture of extra-virgin olive oil, flavored vinegar, mustard and garlic.

For your entrée, serve up a plateful of heart-protecting omega-3 fatty acids—in the form of salmon, swordfish, bluefin tuna or trout. Grill it, bake it or poach it and serve the fish with a yogurt sauce containing dill, horseradish or basil.

Accompany your fish with a medley of steamed vegetables. Broccoli can't be beat for its complement of health-building nutrients. Carrots, sweet peppers and winter squashes are also excellent choices. Flavor your vegetables with a spicy ginger-mustard sauce. Round out the whole plate with brown rice and a few slices of whole-wheat garlic toast topped with herbed tomatoes.

Now you've earned your dessert. How about a Coffee Cup Soufflé? Or a slice of Four Berry Pie? Or some Amaretti Pudding? Say, doesn't that piece of Peach Upside-Down Cake have your name on it. . . .

Jean Rogers

JEAN ROGERS
Food Editor
Prevention Magazine Health Books

INTRODUCTION

꙳ ꙳ ꙳

Trend-spotters have detected an interesting new behavior pattern among Americans: When dining out, many people order an exemplary low-fat meal (broiled, not fried, hold the sauce, and may I have the salad dressing on the side?), and then go on to finish the evening with the most extravagant dessert on the menu—something along the lines of Irresistibly Decadent Triple-Death Chocolate Mousse Cake Pie. This reveals two interesting things: Americans are, indeed, concerned about their fat intake and are trying to eat in a more healthful fashion—which is certainly good news. On the other hand, many people are totally unwilling to give up the lifelong habit of eating something gooey, sweet and high in fat for dessert—even if it means sacrificing other, more nourishing foods elsewhere in their diets.

Wouldn't it be wonderful if there were a way to enjoy well-balanced, nutritious and satisfying meals while still holding to the belief that "something sweet makes the meal complete"? Well, there is, and you're holding it in your hands: a collection of recipes for scrumptious, guilt-free desserts. In this volume are cakes, cookies, puddings, tarts, sorbets, soufflés, crisps, crumbles, compotes and more—old standbys as well as innovative ideas, family favorites along with elegant dinner-party desserts. The fat content has been trimmed but none of the rich goodness sacrificed. And the recipes are straightforward: You won't find yourself stuck in the kitchen for hours, fiddling and fussing with overcomplicated techniques. Many of these recipes are simple enough for kids to help with, and the promise of fresh, hot cookies is a sure way to lure them into the kitchen!

As you try these recipes, you'll discover some ingenious tricks for making healthier desserts. For instance, you can often substitute cocoa powder for solid baking

chocolate, cutting considerable fat in the process (the chocoholics will never guess as they swoon over the Devil's Food Cake and Chocolate-Banana Tart). And did you know that you can replace all or part of the butter or shortening in baked goods with low-fat or fat-free ingredients? Yogurt is the fat-saving substitute in the moist Lemon-Lime Cake and in the tender Spiced Carrot Cake, while applesauce does the trick in the butterscotchy Blondies and old-fashioned Chewy Oatmeal-Apricot Cookies.

Some of the recipes are based on traditional desserts made with egg whites only: The cloud-light Angel Cake with Chocolate Sauce and impressive Strawberry Meringue Tart are two mouth-watering examples. And you can often use egg whites instead of whole eggs: This trick is undetectable in the delicate and delicious Lemon Drop Cookies. Cornstarch, rather than cream, can thicken fruit sauces, and reduced-fat foods—nonfat and reduced-fat sour creams, skim and low-fat milks, nonfat yogurt, reduced-fat and fat-free cream cheeses and reduced-calorie margarine—are also superb "secret ingredients" for healthy dessert making. (Be sure to check that what you're buying is exactly what the recipe calls for: The fat content of reduced-calorie margarine, which varies considerably from brand to brand, can make a big difference in the texture of cookies or pastries.)

Of course, one of the simplest ways to end a meal on a sweet but healthy note is to focus on fruit. Many of the desserts in this book were created with fruit as the main ingredient. In the first section of the book you'll find a useful guide to choosing and using both familiar and exotic fruits; directions for basic fruit preparation as well as some dressier presentation ideas; and a collection of quick, easy fruit sauces that should inspire you to create some delicious desserts of your own.

Buying and Storing Guide for Familiar Fruits

APPLES Some 2,500 varieties of apples are grown in the United States—but you're lucky if you find five different varieties in your local market. The most popular apples, such as Red Delicious and McIntosh, have all but eclipsed interesting older types, such as Newtown Pippins, York Imperials and Winesaps. But there's a movement afoot to revive some of the old varieties, and you may find them at an orchard or a farmers' market. Choosing good apples isn't difficult if you know which varieties are best for various uses. Golden Delicious, Jonathan, Stayman, York, Cortland, Northern Spy and Rhode Island Greening, for instance, are all excellent for cooking. Rome Beauties and Yorks hold their shape when baked whole, while Gravenstein, Golden Delicious, Jonathan and Empire apples make great sauce. For eating raw, try a tart, extra-crisp Macoun or a tangy Winesap. Come autumn, it's fun to buy a selection of apples and have a "tasting" to discover

some new favorites. Always choose hard, unblemished apples that have been kept chilled. Apples are picked when they are fully ripe and ready to be eaten, and if not kept cold, they'll quickly begin to decay, rapidly turning mushy and tasteless. Store apples in a plastic bag in the refrigerator; they'll keep for up to six weeks.

BERRIES Delectable berries are among the most expensive and perishable fruits, so you'll want to choose and store them carefully. Strawberries, raspberries, blackberries and blueberries are best when eaten as soon as possible after picking. Examine the box to be sure that the bottom berries are not moldy or mashed; if you're not using the berries immediately, turn them out onto a paper towel and pick them over, discarding any that are beginning to spoil. Don't wash berries until you're ready to eat

them, and a quick rinse will do. Delicate berries can be safely frozen if they are first spread (unwashed) in a shallow pan and frozen until rock-hard, then transferred to freezer bags. Cranberries are sturdier: Buy a couple of bags at Thanksgiving, when these berries are widely available, and just toss them in the freezer as is. Before cooking the berries, dump them into a bowl of water and remove any leaves, twigs or other debris that float to the top.

CITRUS FRUITS Oranges, lemons, limes, tangerines and grapefruits are semitropical fruits we've come to think of as everyday fare (oranges have been grown in Florida since the early 19th century). Their lively sweet-tart flavors are reason enough to eat these fruits, but as a bonus, all citrus fruits are exceptionally rich in vitamin C. Oranges, tangerines and grapefruits make great snacks, and all citrus fruits yield delicious juices (for a change, mix orange juice with tangerine, lemon or lime juice). Choose well- shaped, smooth, glossy citrus fruits and heft them in your hand: They should feel heavy for their size. Citrus fruits keep longest (several weeks) when refrigerated, but yield more juice at room temperature or warmer. To get the most juice, you can microwave a chilled orange, grapefruit or lemon for about 45 seconds before squeezing it.

GRAPES A big, healthy bunch of grapes makes a classic, elegant dessert. Most grapes you'll find in American markets are European varieties—thin-skinned and seedless or with small, easily removed seeds. American grape varieties are sometimes sold locally (or grown in backyard grape arbors): The most famous is the Concord, used for jelly and juice. American grapes have thick skins that slip off readily, but it's difficult to separate their large seeds from the pulp. It's easy to select good grapes: Look for plump fruits with the silvery "bloom" that signals freshness, and avoid any soft, bruised or shriveled  grapes. Also check the stems: They should be moist and flexible, not brittle, and if you shake the bunch gently, single grapes should not fall off. Color is an indicator of sweetness: Red varieties should have a rich crimson glow; green grapes should be a translucent yellow-green rather than opaque greenish-white. Black grapes should be a deep midnight blue. Store grapes in a plastic bag in the refrigerator for up to one week; give them a quick rinse before serving.

MELONS Watermelon, cantaloupe and honeydew are the most popular melons, but don't overlook the crenshaw, casaba and Santa Claus varieties, or cantaloupe-like Persians and bright yellow Juan Canary melons—all nectar-sweet and delicious. Choosing a good melon can be a challenge: A slight depression at the stem end means that the melon was picked at the proper time, and most varieties exude a sweet fragrance when ripe. Cantaloupes should be golden yellow under their green netting; crenshaws and casabas should also tend toward yellow rather than green. Honeydews should have a velvety, creamy-yellow skin. Watermelons should have a waxy "bloom," and the underside should be yellowish rather than greenish. If you're buying a cut piece, look for one with dense, evenly colored flesh free of white streaks; the seeds should be dark. Store watermelons in the refrigerator; other varieties may need a few days at room temperature to become softer and juicier (although they won't get sweeter).

PEACHES AND NECTARINES These two closely related summer fruits (the nectarine is a subspecies of the peach) are generally interchangeable in dessert recipes, although nectarines are often sweeter than peaches. Both peaches and nectarines may be either freestone or clingstone; the former is easier to halve and peel, and almost all peaches sold fresh are freestones (clingstone peaches are often canned). Nectarines are fuzzless, and nowadays most peaches are defuzzed before they reach the market. Choose fruits with a warm yellow undertone; greenish peaches and nectarines won't be sweet. Even if you purchase fruits that are firm to hard, they will soften (but not sweeten) if left at room temperature for a few days. After ripening, peaches and nectarines can be refrigerated for three to five days.

PEARS A welcome sign of autumn, pears come in a variety of shapes, flavors and textures. But you must exercise a little patience if you want to enjoy pears at their best: These fruits are always picked unripe (so they can withstand the rigors of shipping) and must be allowed a few days at room temperature to soften (unlike melons or peaches, pears will also become sweeter during this time). Bartlett and Comice pears are among the sweetest pears, with thin skin and butter-soft flesh; the elongated, brown-skinned Bosc retains a slight crispness even when ripe. Small Seckel pears, often found at farm markets, are very sweet when ripe, while the ever-popular Anjou is somewhat bland by comparison. Once pears are ripe, store them, loosely wrapped, in the refrigerator and eat them within a few days.

PLUMS There's a rainbow range of plums to choose from, but most of the varieties fit into one of two categories: Japanese or European. The juicy Japanese plums—all of which are clingstones and more or less round—include early-season Red Beauts and Santa Rosas, midsummer's El Dorados and Larodas and late-season Friars and Kelseys. Purple Italian plums (also known as prune plums) are freestone fruits. Sweet and easy to eat, they are also excellent for cook-ing and baking. Plums, like pears, need a little ripening time after they're picked. Choose specimens that are slightly soft at the tip, and keep them at room temperature for a few days; refrigerate once ripe.

An Introduction to Uncommon Fruits

CARAMBOLAS (STAR FRUITS) Slice a carambola crosswise and you get perfect, luminous golden stars—enchanting in a fruit salad and the perfect garnish for platters and beverages. Carambolas grow in tropical countries all over the world, but most of the fruit available here is from Florida. The fruits may be sweet or quite tart (use the tart ones instead of lemons as a garnish): You'll have to sample  the varieties available at your market to discover which type they are. Buy firm fruits with plump ribs; avoid shriveled or browning fruits. Leave carambolas at room temperature until fragrant, then refrigerate.

FIGS Highly perishable and comparatively expensive (they're usually sold individually rather than by the pound), figs are a delectable treat: Their thin skins enclose moist, sweet flesh filled with tiny, crunchy seeds. Most of the fig crop is dried, but you  can find fresh figs in fancy produce stores from June through October. Greenish-yellow Kadotas and deep purple Black Mission figs are the ones most often sold fresh. Although figs are packed carefully, do inspect them well: They should be tender but not mushy, and free of bruises or soft spots. Figs keep for just a few days, and can be stored at room temperature or, if they are ripe, in the refrigerator.

GUAVAS Guavas are a rare treat (their season is brief and the supply is small), so seize the opportunity if they appear at your market. There are many varieties of guavas; some of the more common ones are about the size and shape of large lemons. Their smooth skins may be green or yellow and their flesh varies from white to salmon-pink; the tiny seeds are edible. Choose guavas that give slightly to gentle pressure and be sure they have a sweet fragrance; leave them at room temperature until the aroma becomes strong and perfumy (check often—some varieties can ripen quite abruptly). Don't refrigerate guavas until they are completely ripe. To eat guavas raw, just peel and slice them; or bake the slices for about half an hour. Baked or sautéed guava slices also make a nice accompaniment for poultry.

KIWANOS (HORNED MELONS) A whole kiwano looks like a spiky, red-orange blimp: Cut it open and you'll see shockingly bright, lime-green flesh, studded with seeds. You can halve the fruit lengthwise and scoop out its delicately sweet pulp (seeds and all) with a spoon, or use  the pulp as a topping for frozen yogurt or fruit sorbet. Choose unblemished kiwanos and store them in a cool, dry place (don't refrigerate them). With their hard, shell-like rind, they'll keep for as long as six months.

KIWIFRUITS These Chinese natives have now become a major crop in New Zealand and California. Thanks to complementary growing seasons in the Northern and Southern hemispheres, kiwifruits are widely available all year round. These furry-skinned brown fruits are roughly the size and shape of extra-large eggs; their emerald-green flesh, with its starburst pattern of small, crunchy black seeds, has a flavor that's often described as a cross between strawberry, melon and banana. Choose unbruised kiwifruits; if they're very firm, let them ripen for a few days at room temperature and then place them in a plastic bag and refrigerate them. Kiwifruits serve as great snacks. Sliced or diced kiwifruits are an excellent addition to fruit salads and they make a pretty topping for a tart (see pages 104–105). For more information on kiwifruits, see pages 14–15.

MANGOES This luscious fruit's velvety orange-yellow flesh is intensely sweet and juicy. Mangoes are about the same size as apples, with a slightly irregular oval shape and a large, flat pit. The Tommy Atkins variety is the most widely available, but ask the produce manager about Haden, Kent and Keitt mangoes, which are tastier, with smoother flesh. Mangoes with a touch of yellow or red will ripen to full sweetness; gray-green fruits will not. Even an unripe mango should have a floral fragrance; avoid fruits that smell even slightly of alcohol or turpentine. Ripen mangoes at room temperature for a few days, or until their color and fragrance develop and the fruit gives a bit when squeezed between your palms. It's best to eat a mango as soon as it's ripe— by itself or as a salad ingredient. (For information on preparing mangoes, see pages 14–15.)

PAPAYAS Most papayas come to our markets from Hawaii, with a small proportion grown in Florida. The more familiar varieties, such as the Solo, are pear-shaped; the Solo weighs about one pound, but other varieties can be much larger. The papaya's  greenish-yellow skin surrounds golden-yellow or pink flesh; the central cavity is filled with peppery-tasting edible seeds. Choose fruits that are at least partially yellow, and leave them at room temperature (away from direct light, if possible) until they are as tender as ripe avocados. Refrigerate ripe papayas if you won't be using them right away. You can eat a halved papaya from its skin, or add the diced flesh to fruit salads; use puréed papaya in dessert sauces and salad dressings. Or, try the purée as a marinade—it's a natural meat tenderizer.

PASSION FRUITS The pitted exterior of these unattractive little fruits hide a deliciously perfumy treat. When ripe, these egg-sized treasures are a dusty yellow or purple (depending on the variety), their tough skins dented and wrinkled. The interior is not much more appealing—a custardy, dull yellow pulp laced with seeds. But if you persevere, either to spoon the fruit from the shell or squeeze its juice, you'll be rewarded with a sublime honeyed floral flavor. Choose largish, heavy passion fruits, which will be juiciest; if they're smooth, keep them at room temperature until the rind shrivels and the fruit softens. Then refrigerate the fruit for up to a week or freeze, whole and well wrapped, for several months.

PERSIMMONS Although wild persimmons grow in the United States, those sold in American markets are Japanese varieties. These plum-sized, burnt-orange fruits have smooth, sweet flesh that's often completely seedless. There's an important distinction between the two most popular persimmon varieties: You can bite  into a tomato-shaped Fuyu as you would an apple— the fruit is sweet even when firm. But one bite of an unripe acorn-shaped Hachiya will induce a powerful pucker. When ripe, Hachiyas are so soft they must be eaten with a spoon. Choose firm, unblemished persimmons with bright, even color—firm Fuyus for immediate enjoyment, and slightly softer Hachiyas for home ripening, which takes about a week. Store ripe persimmons in the refrigerator or wrap and freeze the whole fruits for up to three months.

POMEGRANATES These softball-sized fruits usually appear in the fall, remaining available throughout the winter. Pomegranates are not candidates for casual munching, as the edible portion, which con-  sists of ruby-colored kernels, is surrounded by a tough shell and a network of pith. But it's worth a little trouble to enjoy the sweet-tart taste of the jewel-like kernels. Select large, heavy specimens with shiny skins; you can store pomegranates for up to three months in the refrigerator. (For detailed information on preparing and using pomegranates, see pages 14–15.)

Preparation of Familiar Fruits

CORING AND SLICING APPLES

When you're using apples in quantity for a pie, a crisp or a big batch of applesauce, preparing the fruit can become a bit of a chore. Specialized tools for peeling, coring and slicing are inexpensive; begin with a good-quality swivel-bladed peeler (unless you're adept at peeling with a paring knife) and consider using the gadgets shown here for easier coring.

Center this sturdy corer-slicer over a peeled or unpeeled apple and push down firmly: The fruit will be simultaneously cored and cut into eight wedges.

PEELING AND SLICING A PINEAPPLE

A pineapple can be an intimidating fruit: Bristling with spiky leaves and armored with a tough shell, it looks difficult to peel and core. But if you have a sharp, heavy knife, you're halfway to turning out thick, juicy slices of this delectable fruit. A small cookie cutter is the perfect tool for cutting the core from each slice.

To remove the leaves, cut across the top of the pineapple. Cut a slice from the bottom so that the fruit will stand steady.

PEELING AND SEGMENTING AN ORANGE

Navel oranges are easy to peel and section, but juice oranges are trickier to handle. And if you plan to use either type of fruit in a salad or for a garnish, it will be much more pleasant to eat if the tough membranes as well as the bitter white pith have been removed. This method works for grapefruits, too.

Start by cutting a thin slice from the top and bottom of each orange with a sharp knife.

Push this corer through the stem end of an unpeeled apple (it's less slippery), then pull it out to remove the core. Aim carefully, or you may miss part of the core.

A sturdy melon baller is a good tool for removing the core from halved apples; it works well for pears, too.

If you've used the tube-shaped corer, you can then peel the apple and slice it into attractive ring-shaped cross sections.

Stand the pineapple upright and slice downward to remove strips of rind; cut deeply to remove most of the eyes.

Lay the peeled pineapple on the cutting board and cut it crosswise into slices. With a smaller knife, trim any remaining eyes from the slices.

Press a small round cookie cutter or canape cutter into the center of each slice to remove the tough core.

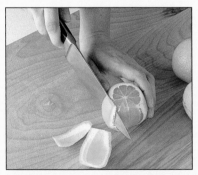

Stand the orange upright and slice downward to remove the rind. Cut away the white pith as well as the colored part of the peel.

Working over a bowl to catch the juice, slide the knife along each side of the membranes to free the segments.

When all the segments have been freed, squeeze the membranes in your hand to release any remaining juice.

Preparation of Uncommon Fruits

How to Handle a Mango

It has been suggested that the only sensible place to eat a mango is in the bathtub: This fruit is so juicy, and the flesh clings so tightly to the large, flat pit, that it's hard not to make a mess of it. There is, however, a straightforward and practical method of cutting up and peeling a mango. A sharp knife is essential.

Hold the mango vertically and slice down either side of the pit to remove two fleshy "cheeks" of flesh.

Preparing Kiwifruits

Its vivid green color and pretty starburst of seeds make the kiwifruit a natural as a garnish, and this egg-sized wonder is also one of the best fruit sources of vitamin C and potassium. You can eat a kiwi-fruit as you would a peach (rub off the fuzz first), but since the skin is a bit leathery, you may want to peel or "shell" it first.

To pare a kiwifruit, first cut a slice off the top so the peeler can get a grip on the edge of the rather thick skin.

Extracting Pomegranate Seeds

Clusters of potassium-rich pomegranate seeds are treasures hidden within a tough skin and thick pith. Put the whole kernels in your mouth, savor the fruit and either swallow or spit out the crunchy insides. Scatter pomegranate kernels atop a fruit salad or a dish of sorbet, or use them to garnish party platters. You can also crush the kernels to yield a delicious juice (see right), but beware: The juice stains indelibly.

Don an apron so you don't risk staining your clothes, then cut out a small cone-shaped section from the blossom end of the fruit.

Score the flesh into cubes, and then press the skin side upward: The cubes will pop up, and you can slice them off the skin.

With a small knife or a vegetable peeler, remove the skin from the portion of flesh still attached to the pit.

Make a few cuts toward the pit through the flesh, then slice around the pit to remove the flesh in fairly large pieces.

To quarter or dice the kiwifruit, first halve the fruit crosswise and then scoop out each half with a tablespoon.

To make little kiwifruit balls: Halve an unpeeled fruit and use the small end of a melon baller to turn out tiny spheres.

These berry-sized "hardy kiwis" grow in cooler climates than the larger fruits. Just cut them in half for an edible garnish. (You can eat the skin, too.)

Score the fruit into quarters through the skin and pith, but don't cut too deeply or you'll pierce the fleshy kernels.

Pull the fruit apart, then gently push out the kernels with your fingers. It's tedious work, but worth the effort.

For juice, roll and press the fruit with your hands: you'll hear the kernels burst inside. Then pierce deeply with a metal skewer or paring knife to release the juice.

Fruit Servers and Garnishes

MAKING LEMON (OR ORANGE) CUPS

Bright citrus cups make attractive containers for condiments (such as cranberry sauce) or desserts (pack fruit sorbet into the cups, then freeze them and top with their own "caps"). Squeeze the scooped-out flesh and use the juice for cooking.

Cut off the pointed end of the lemon; discard it or save it to use as a "cap" to set atop the completed cup.

MAKING A MELON BASKET

A watermelon, cantaloupe or honeydew can be carved into a basket for serving fruit salad; a small "icebox" watermelon is just the right size for a small party. Start by standing the melon stem-end up and drawing a line around its "belt" to guide you in making a level cut; mark the shape of the handle, too.

Make your first cut halfway through the melon, slightly to one side of the center, to form one side of the handle.

MAKING CITRUS TWISTS

Fruit cups taste zestier and drinks seem cooler when garnished with slices of lime, lemon or orange. These jaunty citrus twists are given their stripes with a gadget called a channel knife, which you can find in kitchenware stores. You can make the twists ahead of time up to the point of notching the slices, then refrigerate them until needed. Use the strips of zest you remove as an additional garnish, or freeze them for later use in recipes.

Holding the fruit in your hand and pressing firmly with the knife, scrape from bottom to top to remove strips of peel.

With a sharp paring knife, cut around inside the white pith to loosen the pulp in a cylindrical shape.

Insert the knife tip into the bottom of the lemon; without cutting off the bottom, gently wiggle the knife to free the pulp.

Use a tablespoon to remove the cylinder of pulp; then cut a thin slice off the bottom so the lemon can stand without toppling.

Make a second, parallel cut to define the handle, then make a perpendicular cut to form the surface of the basket. Remove the wedge of melon and set aside.

Cut along the underside of the handle with a smaller knife, then cut across the surface to release this section of flesh.

Remove the melon flesh with a large spoon or, if you prefer, scoop it out with a melon baller.

When you've cut a series of strips at equally spaced intervals around the fruit, slice it crosswise.

Cut a notch in each slice from the center to one edge. If making the twists in advance, squeeze some juice over them and store in a covered container.

At serving time, hold each slice on either side of the notch and twist the sides in opposite directions.

Fruit Sauces and Syrups

Here are four true-fruit toppings that will establish your reputation as a master of desserts. Keep these intensely flavorful sauces and syrups on hand (or whip them up on the spot) to serve warm or cold over fresh fruits, low-fat cakes, waffles or pancakes, yogurt or frozen desserts.

RASPBERRY SAUCE

❧ ❧ ❧

This ruby red sauce is striking and tasty when served with orangy-yellow fruits—sliced mango, papaya, cantaloupe or oranges. It's also the perfect complement to the Lemon-Lime Cake (page 100). When raspberries are in season, make a double recipe and freeze the extra sauce.

> 2 **cups fresh raspberries**
>
> 3 **tablespoons granulated sugar**
>
> 2 **tablespoons water**
>
> 1 **tablespoon light corn syrup**

1 In a food processor, combine the raspberries, sugar, water and corn syrup, and process until puréed.

2 Press the mixture through a fine strainer suspended over a medium bowl to remove the seeds.

3 Use immediately, or place in a covered glass container and refrigerate for up to a week.

Per tablespoon 20 calories, 0.1 g. fat, 0 g. saturated fat, 0 mg. cholesterol, 2 mg. sodium **Makes 1 cup**

CHUNKY STRAWBERRY SAUCE

❧ ❧ ❧

Celebrate summer with a bowl of blueberries topped with this fragrant sauce and a dollop of plain yogurt, or spoon the strawberry sauce over lemon sorbet or vanilla frozen yogurt. Drizzle the sauce over slices of lightly toasted angel food cake or spread some onto toasted English muffins for an instant shortcake.

> 3 **cups whole strawberries**
>
> 3 **tablespoons granulated sugar**
>
> 1 **tablespoon fresh lemon juice**

1 Hull and thinly slice the strawberries; place in a medium bowl. Sprinkle with the sugar and stir to combine. Cover with plastic wrap and let stand at room temperature for 20 minutes, or until the juices begin to flow.

2 With a potato masher, mash the strawberries to a chunky consistency. Stir in the lemon juice.

3 Use immediately, or place in a covered glass container and refrigerate for up to a week.

Per tablespoon 12 calories, 0.1 g. fat, 0 g. saturated fat, 0 mg. cholesterol, 0 mg. sodium **Makes 1½ cups**

ORANGE-CINNAMON SYRUP

❧ ❧ ❧

Orange sections macerated in this spicy syrup and served in glass goblets make an elegant finale for a dinner party; accompany the fruit with crisp cookies. Or, drizzle the syrup over crêpes or slices of fat-free pound cake.

2 **large navel oranges**

1½ **cups water**

½ **cup packed light brown sugar**

3 **tablespoons frozen orange juice concentrate**

½ **cinnamon stick**

1 Grate 1½ teaspoons of zest from one of the oranges. Reserve the orange.

2 In a medium, heavy saucepan, combine the water, sugar, orange juice concentrate and grated orange zest, and stir until the sugar dissolves. Add the cinnamon stick and bring to a boil over medium-high heat. Reduce the heat to medium-low, cover and simmer for 5 minutes.

3 Meanwhile, working over a small bowl, peel and section the oranges (see pages 12–13). Place the orange sections on a cutting board and cut each in half crosswise. Squeeze the juice from the membranes into the bowl.

4 Remove the cinnamon stick from the syrup. Add the orange juice, cover and simmer for 5 minutes longer. Stir in the orange sections and remove the pan from the heat. Cover and let steep for 5 minutes. Use immediately, or store in a covered glass container in the refrigerator for up to 2 weeks.

Per tablespoon 14 calories, 0 g. fat, 0 g. saturated fat, 0 mg. cholesterol, 1 mg. sodium **Makes 3 cups**

BLUEBERRY-LEMON MAPLE SYRUP

❧ ❧ ❧

Two breakfast favorites are combined in this sweet berry syrup, which is good either hot or cold. Pour it over buckwheat pancakes or waffles (waffles make a fine dessert). Easier still, just stir a spoonful of syrup into a cup of vanilla yogurt.

1½ **cups maple syrup**

½ **cup water**

¼ **cup fresh lemon juice**

Two 2-inch strips lemon zest

¼ **teaspoon ground nutmeg**

⅛ **teaspoon vanilla extract**

1½ **cups fresh blueberries**

1 In a medium, heavy saucepan, combine the maple syrup, water, lemon juice, lemon zest, nutmeg and vanilla, and bring to a boil over medium-high heat. Reduce the heat to low, cover and simmer for 10 minutes. Remove the lemon zest.

2 Stir in the blueberries, remove from the heat, cover and let steep for 5 minutes to blend the flavors.

3 Use immediately, or store in a covered glass container in the refrigerator for up to 2 weeks. Reheat, if desired, before serving.

Per tablespoon 29 calories, 0 g. fat, 0 g. saturated fat, 0 mg. cholesterol, 1 mg. sodium **Makes 3 cups**

Cool Delights

❧ ❧ ❧

SPARKLING SORBETS,
CHILLED PUDDINGS, SHIMMERING
GELATIN DESSERTS AND COLD
COMPOTES TO REFRESH THE PALATE

GINGERED CANTALOUPE SORBET

1 **large ripe cantaloupe, peeled, seeded and cut into chunks (about 4 cups)**

½ **cup sugar**

2 **tablespoons light corn syrup**

1 **tablespoon fresh lemon juice**

1 **tablespoon peeled grated fresh ginger**

2 **tablespoons minced crystallized ginger**

Mint sprigs, for garnish (optional)

Fine-quality crystallized ginger comes in good-size chunks and slices.

Y ou don't need an ice-cream machine to make sorbet—just a food processor—and you can produce flavors you'll never find at the supermarket, like this sublime gingered melon ice. It contains both pungent fresh ginger and sweet-hot crystallized ginger—lively accents to the fragrant sweetness of the melon.

1 Place the cantaloupe, sugar, corn syrup, lemon juice and fresh ginger in a food processor, and process until smooth. Add the crystallized ginger and pulse just until mixed. Pour into a 9 x 9-inch metal baking pan, cover with foil and freeze for at least 6 hours, or overnight, or until frozen hard.

2 Remove the sorbet from the freezer and let stand for a few minutes until softened. Break the sorbet into chunks. In batches, place the sorbet in a food processor and pulse until creamy and smooth.

3 Transfer the sorbet to a freezer container, cover and freeze for at least 1 hour, or until you are ready to serve.

4 To serve, soften at room temperature for a few minutes. Spoon the sorbet into 4 dessert dishes or goblets. Garnish with mint sprigs, if desired.

Preparation time 10 minutes • **Total time** 20 minutes plus chilling time • **Per serving** 211 calories, 0.5 g. fat (2% of calories), 0 g. saturated fat, 0 mg. cholesterol, 32 mg. sodium, 1.3 g. dietary fiber, 37 mg. calcium, 2 mg. iron, 73 mg. vitamin C, 3.1 mg. beta-carotene • **Serves 4**

MARKET AND PANTRY
Crystallized ginger is made by cooking slices of fresh ginger in a sugar syrup, then coating it with granulated sugar. This turns the ginger into a tasty confection with a consistency like that of firm dried fruit. The crystallized ginger sold in small jars in supermarket spice racks can be very expensive. Better bets are gourmet or candy shops, or Asian markets, where the ginger is sold by the pound. It's usually much cheaper and also of better quality.

Preceding pages: Poached Peaches with Raspberries (recipe on page 44)

FRESH FRUIT TERRINE

1 envelope plus 1 teaspoon
unflavored gelatin

½ cup cold water

2 cups cranberry juice cocktail

3 tablespoons sugar

3 medium nectarines, cut into thin
wedges (about 3 cups)

1¾ cups sliced fresh strawberries

Nectarine slices and halved
strawberries, for garnish
(optional)

For smooth slices, use a thin serrated knife
and dip the blade into hot water before
making each cut.

There's just no comparison, in terms of flavor, between this "stained-glass" dessert and one made from a boxed dessert mix. However, the method and preparation time are pretty much the same, so why not start from scratch? The slices of nectarine and berries are so pretty that you don't need to use a fancy mold—a simple loaf pan will do. This gives the dessert the shape of a classic French *terrine*, and makes turning it out of the mold easier, too.

1 Spray an 8 x 4-inch loaf pan with no-stick spray.

2 In a medium metal bowl, sprinkle the gelatin over the cold water and let stand for 2 minutes to soften.

3 In a small saucepan, combine the cranberry juice cocktail and sugar, and bring to a boil over high heat, stirring to dissolve the sugar. Pour the boiling juice mixture over the softened gelatin and stir until the gelatin is completely dissolved.

4 Place the bowl with the cranberry-gelatin mixture over a larger bowl of ice water and let sit, stirring occasionally, for 8 to 10 minutes, or until the mixture is cold and just starts to jell. Stir in the fruits and turn the mixture into the prepared loaf pan. Cover with plastic wrap and chill for at least 6 hours, or overnight, until set.

5 To unmold, dip the pan briefly into a basin of hot water and invert over a platter. Shake to loosen the terrine, then remove the pan.

6 If desired, surround the terrine with nectarine slices and halved strawberries, or cut the terrine into 8 slices, place a slice on each of 8 dessert plates and garnish each serving with the fresh fruits.

Preparation time 10 minutes • **Total time** 30 minutes plus chilling time • **Per serving** 94 calories, 0.5 g. fat (5% of calories), 0 g. saturated fat, 0 mg. cholesterol, 4 mg. sodium, 1.7 g. dietary fiber, 10 mg. calcium, 0 mg. iron, 44 mg. vitamin C, 0.2 mg. beta-carotene • **Serves 8**

Fruit Compote with Pound Cake

1 cup water

½ cup apple juice

1 medium Golden Delicious apple, peeled, quartered and cut into ½-inch wedges

1 medium pear, peeled, cored and cut into ¾-inch chunks

⅓ cup dried apricot halves

⅓ cup halved pitted prunes

3 tablespoons packed dark brown sugar

2 tablespoons golden raisins

1 large lemon

¼ teaspoon ground nutmeg

1 bay leaf, preferably imported

One (13.6-ounce) fat-free pound cake

A combination of fresh and dried fruits, this nutmeg-spiced compote captures the essence of autumn. Served over fat-free pound cake, it makes a remarkably nutritious dessert. For a change, spoon the compote over fat-free frozen yogurt or a slice of warm homemade gingerbread; or present the mixture in goblets with crisp gingersnaps on the side.

1 In a large, heavy saucepan, combine the water, apple juice, apples, pears, apricots, prunes, sugar and raisins.

2 Cut the lemon in half, then cut one half into thin slices. Cut the slices in half crosswise. Squeeze enough juice from the other lemon half into a small bowl to measure 2 tablespoons.

3 Add the lemon slices, lemon juice, nutmeg and bay leaf to the fruit mixture, and stir to combine. Bring to a simmer over medium-high heat. Reduce the heat to medium-low, cover and continue to simmer for 15 to 20 minutes, or until the fruits are very tender.

4 Pour the mixture into a medium bowl, cover and chill until ready to serve. Remove the bay leaf.

5 Just before serving, cut the pound cake into eight ¾-inch-thick slices. Place a slice of cake on each of 8 dessert plates. Spoon about ⅓ cup of the compote over each slice.

Preparation time 10 minutes • **Total time** 40 minutes plus chilling time • **Per serving** 218 calories, 0.3 g. fat (1% of calories), 0 g. saturated fat, 0 mg. cholesterol, 167 mg. sodium, 2.6 g. dietary fiber, 27 mg. calcium, 1 mg. iron, 21 mg. vitamin C, 0.4 mg. beta-carotene • **Serves 8**

NUTRITION NOTE
A box or bag of dried fruits is a "prize package," nutritionally speaking. Prunes are one of the best sources of fiber and supply lots of beta-carotene, iron, potassium and B vitamins as well. Dried apricots are an outstanding source of beta-carotene and a good source of iron. Although grapes are not tremendously nutritious, drying them concentrates their nutrients; in fact, raisins supply good amounts of iron, potassium and fiber.

SUMMER FRUITS WITH SPICED YOGURT

1½ cups plain nonfat yogurt

½ medium cantaloupe

2 large nectarines

3 large plums

½ cup halved red seedless grapes

2 tablespoons honey

⅛ teaspoon ground cardamom

8 drops rosewater or almond extract

The delicate fragrance of the yogurt sauce may be familiar to lovers of Indian cuisine. The thickened yogurt is blended with cardamom and rosewater, two ingredients featured in many Indian sweets: Whole cardamom pods or ground cardamom seeds flavor coconut pudding and coconut fudge as well as hot tea, and rosewater lends a delicate perfume to rice pudding, cashew fudge and *lassi*—a yogurt "milkshake."

1 Line a strainer with cheesecloth or a double layer of paper towels and place the strainer over a medium bowl. Spoon the yogurt into the strainer and let drain for 20 minutes. Discard the whey, wipe out the bowl and spoon the yogurt into the bowl.

2 While the yogurt is draining, peel and seed the cantaloupe, and cut it into bite-size chunks. Place the cantaloupe in a medium serving bowl. Slice the nectarines and plums, and add to the cantaloupe. Add the grapes and stir to combine.

3 Add the honey, cardamom and rosewater or almond extract to the drained yogurt, and whisk to blend.

4 Drizzle the fruits with some of the spiced yogurt and serve the rest of the yogurt on the side.

After spooning the yogurt into the cheese-cloth-lined strainer, stir the yogurt to break it up a bit and start the whey separating.

Preparation time 5 minutes • **Total time** 30 minutes • **Per serving** 116 calories, 0.7 g. fat (5% of calories), 0 g. saturated fat, 0 mg. cholesterol, 24 mg. sodium, 2.3 g. dietary fiber, 81 mg. calcium, 0 mg. iron, 25 mg. vitamin C, 1.1 mg. beta-carotene • **Serves 6**

MARKET AND PANTRY
Rosewater is made from roses specially grown for their fragrance. It is sold in gourmet shops, Middle Eastern stores and many pharmacies.

SUBSTITUTION
If you're unable to get rosewater, or don't care for it, use almond extract instead. Be sure to buy pure almond extract—the imitation type has a distinctly inferior flavor.

RHUBARB-STRAWBERRY COMPOTE

⅓ cup strawberry all-fruit
  preserves

¼ cup sugar

2 tablespoons water

3 cups sliced rhubarb, cut into
  2-inch pieces (about 12 ounces)

3 cups thinly sliced strawberries

  Mint sprigs, for garnish
  (optional)

Stewed rhubarb and strawberries make up the ever-popular fill-ing for an early-summer pie (rhubarb is sometimes called "pie plant"); the combination offers a pleasing balance of sweet and tart. However, some standard recipes call for 2 to 3 cups of sugar—with almost sickeningly sweet results. Here, strawberry all-fruit preserves are used in the compote, so only ¼ cup of granulated sugar is needed. And if you save this recipe until local strawberries are in season, you'll find that they add plenty of their own sweetness.

1 In a medium, heavy nonreactive saucepan, combine the preserves, sugar and water, and whisk until smooth. Add the rhubarb and stir to coat. Bring to a simmer over medium heat. Reduce the heat to medium-low, cover and continue to simmer gently, turning the rhubarb occasionally with a rubber spatula so it stays intact, for 10 to 12 min-utes, or until the rhubarb is very tender.

2 Remove the mixture from the heat and pour into a serving bowl or 4 dessert glasses. With a rubber spatula, gently fold in the straw-berries. Cover with vented plastic wrap and chill for 1 hour, or until ready to serve. Garnish with mint sprigs, if desired.

Preparation time 5 minutes • **Total time** 50 minutes plus chilling time • **Per serving** 156 calories, 0.6 g. fat (3% of calories), 0 g. saturated fat, 0 mg. cholesterol, 5 mg. sodium, 3 g. dietary fiber, 89 mg. calcium, 1 mg. iron, 71 mg. vitamin C, 0.1 mg. beta-carotene • **Serves 4**

MARKET AND PANTRY
Rhubarb resembles Swiss chard, with its thick, fleshy stalks and fanlike leaves. But while chard is served as a vegetable, rhubarb has come to be unofficially con-sidered a fruit: Though undeniably tart, it is used in desserts, jams and wines. Both hothouse and field-grown rhubarb are available; the color of the field-grown plant—both stems and leaves—is brighter, and the flavor is more intense. Field-grown rhubarb is sold only in the spring, while hothouse rhubarb is available practically all year round. Always remove and discard the leaves: They contain high levels of oxalic acid, which is toxic. You can freeze uncooked rhubarb (cut it into 2-inch pieces first) for six months to a year.

AMARETTI PUDDING

2 cups 1% low-fat milk

⅓ cup packed light brown sugar

¼ cup cornstarch

¼ teaspoon salt

½ cup skim milk

1 teaspoon vanilla extract

5 large amaretti cookies
   (1¼ ounces), crumbled

Velvety desserts like this vanilla pudding need something crunchy for contrast. Here, crumbled *amaretti*—crisp almond-flavored macaroons from Italy—top the pudding. You can find amaretti, in brightly colored tins or bags, at gourmet shops, Italian grocery stores and many supermarkets. If you can't buy them, however, try another crisp topping, such as crumbled chocolate or vanilla wafers, your favorite breakfast cereal or a few spoonfuls of toasted coconut.

1 In a medium, heavy saucepan, warm the low-fat milk over medium heat just until small bubbles form around the edge and the milk is steaming. Remove the pan from the heat and set aside.

2 Meanwhile, in a medium bowl, whisk together the sugar, cornstarch and salt until blended. (You may need to break up the lumps of sugar with your fingers.) Gradually whisk in the skim milk until the mixture is smooth.

3 Pour the reserved low-fat milk into the sugar mixture and whisk until blended. Return the mixture to the saucepan and bring to a boil over medium heat, stirring constantly. Continue to boil, stirring, for 1 minute. Remove from the heat and stir in the vanilla.

4 Ladle the pudding into 4 dessert dishes or glasses, cover and refrigerate for about 1½ hours, or until chilled.

5 Just before serving, sprinkle each pudding with some amaretti crumbs.

Preparation time 10 minutes • **Total time** 30 minutes plus chilling time • **Per serving** 203 calories, 2.3 g. fat (10% of calories), 0.8 g. saturated fat, 6 mg. cholesterol, 224 mg. sodium, 0.1 g. dietary fiber, 204 mg. calcium, 0 mg. iron, 2 mg. vitamin C, 0.2 mg. beta-carotene • **Serves 4**

KITCHEN TIP

As anyone who's ever made gravy knows, cornstarch sometimes forms lumps when stirred into liquid. Combining the cornstarch with the sugar, and then whisking in the milk, helps keep this from happening.

MARGARITA FRUITS

3 cups whole strawberries, hulled
and quartered

2 tablespoons granulated sugar

2 tablespoons frozen orange juice
concentrate

½ teaspoon grated lime zest

2 tablespoons fresh lime juice

1 tablespoon tequila (optional)

3 cups honeydew balls

Lime wedges, raw sugar and
grated lime zest, for garnish
(optional)

The Mexican cocktail called a *margarita* is made from tequila, orange liqueur and lime juice—a potent mixture that belies its innocent name (*margarita* is Spanish for "daisy"). To provide a sharp foil for its fruitiness, the drink is often served in a glass edged with coarse salt. Here, the dessert goblets are edged with raw sugar, available in most supermarkets.

1 In a medium bowl, combine the strawberries and granulated sugar. Let stand for 25 minutes, or until the juices begin to flow.

2 In a small bowl, combine the orange juice concentrate, lime zest, lime juice, and tequila, if using. Add the strawberries and their juice and the honeydew balls, and mix gently with a rubber spatula.

3 If desired, for a traditional margarita presentation, moisten the rims of 4 goblets with lime wedges. Place the raw sugar on a plate and dip the rim of each goblet into the sugar to coat it.

4 Carefully spoon the fruits and juice into the goblets and garnish each serving with lime zest, if desired.

Preparation time 10 minutes • **Total time** 25 minutes • **Per serving** 119 calories, 0.6 g. fat (4% of calories), 0 g. saturated fat, 0 mg. cholesterol, 14 mg. sodium, 4.2 g. dietary fiber, 28 mg. calcium, 1 mg. iron, 111 mg. vitamin C, 0.1 mg. beta-carotene • **Serves 4**

❧ ❧ ❧

Scoop out the seeds and fibers from the honeydew with a tablespoon.

Then insert a melon baller deep into the flesh to make balls that are nearly round.

LIME-MANGO MOLDS WITH FRUIT SAUCE

1 large ripe mango (about 1¼ pounds)

½ cup cold water

¼ cup sugar

3 tablespoons fresh lime juice

2 tablespoons honey

1 envelope unflavored gelatin

1 tablespoon chopped fresh cilantro

1 cup hulled whole strawberries

½ cup fresh raspberries or ½ cup frozen raspberries, thawed

4 strawberries, cut into fans, for garnish (optional)

These individual gelatin desserts glow with the colors of an island sunset. And the mango and lime evoke the flavors of the tropics. A touch of fresh cilantro provides an unexpected accent to the fruits.

1 Spray four 5- to 6-ounce decorative molds, custard cups or small soufflé dishes with no-stick spray.

2 Cut the fruit off the mango (see pages 14–15 for instructions), then place the pieces of mango in a food processor. Add ¼ cup of the cold water, 2 tablespoons of the sugar, the lime juice and honey, and process until puréed. Pour the purée into a medium bowl.

3 In a small saucepan, sprinkle the gelatin over the remaining ¼ cup water and let stand for 2 minutes. Cook the gelatin mixture over low heat, stirring, until the mixture is hot and the gelatin is dissolved.

4 Pour the dissolved gelatin into the mango purée and stir to combine. Stir in the cilantro. Divide the mango purée evenly among the prepared molds. Cover each with plastic wrap and chill for about 2 hours, or until the gelatin is set.

5 Meanwhile, place the whole strawberries, the raspberries and remaining 2 tablespoons sugar in a blender or food processor, and blend or process until puréed. Press the mixture through a fine strainer set over a medium bowl to remove the seeds. Cover and chill until ready to serve.

6 To unmold, briefly rub the outsides of the molds, cups or dishes with a kitchen towel or sponge dipped in hot water and invert over 4 dessert plates. Shake a few times to loosen the gelatin.

7 Spoon the fruit sauce around each gelatin dessert. Place a strawberry fan on top of each, if desired.

Preparation time 5 minutes • **Total time** 30 minutes plus chilling time • **Per serving** 179 calories, 1.5 g. fat (8% of calories), 0.1 g. saturated fat, 0 mg. cholesterol, 7 mg. sodium, 2.8 g. dietary fiber, 21 mg. calcium, 0 mg. iron, 56 mg. vitamin C, 2.3 mg. beta-carotene • **Serves 4**

❧ ❧ ❧

LEMON-MINT WATERMELON GRANITA

3 pounds watermelon, seeded and cut into chunks (about 4 cups)

⅓ cup sugar

⅓ cup fresh lemon juice

2 tablespoons light corn syrup

2 tablespoons slivered mint leaves

¾ teaspoon grated lemon zest

Even colder than a well-chilled watermelon, this refreshing dessert takes the form of a *granita*, a super-crunchy Italian ice. To produce the pleasantly granular texture, periodically stir and scrape the partially frozen mixture with a fork. This technique brings the iciest portions into the less-frozen center and maintains the crystalline quality of the ice.

1 Place the watermelon chunks, sugar, lemon juice and corn syrup in a blender or food processor, in batches if necessary, and process to a smooth purée. Add the slivered mint and lemon zest, and pulse just to mix.

2 Pour the watermelon mixture into a 9-inch square metal baking pan and place in the freezer. Freeze, scraping the frozen edges toward the middle every 30 minutes or so, for 2 to 3 hours, or until the granita is slushy and granular.

3 Cover and freeze for at least 2 to 3 hours longer, or until frozen hard.

4 To serve, scrape the surface of the ice with a metal spoon to create a granular texture, then spoon into 4 goblets or dessert dishes.

Preparation time 15 minutes • **Total time** 25 minutes plus chilling time • **Per serving** 150 calories, 0.7 g. fat (4% of calories), 0 g. saturated fat, 0 mg. cholesterol, 16 mg. sodium, 0.6 g. dietary fiber, 16 mg. calcium, 0 mg. iron, 26 mg. vitamin C, 0.4 mg. beta-carotene • **Serves 4**

MARKET AND PANTRY
You'll find two types of watermelon in the market, at least during the summer: picnic and icebox. Picnic watermelons weigh up to 50 pounds—they're the massive blimp-shaped fruits you'd serve at a barbecue.

Icebox melons are bred to fit into the refrigerator: They're round or oval and weigh from 5 to 10 pounds. Some icebox watermelons are seedless. With its deep-colored, crunchy flesh, a seedless melon would be ideal for this recipe.

POACHED PEACHES WITH RASPBERRIES

2 cups white grape juice

2 cups water

½ cup honey

1 cinnamon stick, broken in half

1 teaspoon allspice berries or
¼ teaspoon ground allspice

4 whole cloves or ⅛ teaspoon
ground cloves

4 large ripe peaches

1 cup fresh raspberries

Use whole allspice berries (left) and cloves (right) to flavor syrups, sauces and beverages; it's easy to strain the spices out after cooking, if necessary.

Dame Nellie Melba, a turn-of-the-century opera singer, inspired the most famous pairing of peaches and raspberries, a dish known to this day as *pêche Melba*. The great French chef Georges Escoffier created the recipe for poached peaches and raspberry sauce served over vanilla ice cream. For this elegant adaptation, the peaches are simmered in a warmly spiced mixture of grape juice, cinnamon, allspice and cloves. You can save the syrup (refrigerate it in a covered jar) and use it to cook other fruits.

1 In a large nonreactive saucepan, combine the grape juice, water, honey, cinnamon stick, allspice and cloves. Cover and bring to a boil over high heat. Reduce the heat to medium and simmer for 5 minutes to blend the flavors.

2 Add the whole peaches, increase the heat to medium-high and bring just to a boil. Reduce the heat to medium, cover and simmer for 20 minutes, or until the peaches are fork-tender. Remove the pan from the heat and let the peaches cool in the pan, uncovered, for 10 minutes.

3 Remove the peaches from the syrup, reserving the syrup. Slip off the skins, halve the peaches and remove the stones.

4 Spoon 1 cup of the syrup into a medium bowl and place the peach halves in the syrup. (Save the remaining syrup for another use.) Cover with vented plastic wrap and chill for about 1 hour, or until ready to serve.

5 To serve, place 2 peach halves in each of 4 dessert dishes. Pour ¼ cup of syrup over each portion and top each with ¼ cup of raspberries.

Preparation time 5 minutes • **Total time** 50 minutes plus chilling time • **Per serving** 152 calories, 0.3 g. fat (2% of calories), 0 g. saturated fat, 0 mg. cholesterol, 2 mg. sodium, 4.1 g. dietary fiber, 21 mg. calcium, 1 mg. iron, 29 mg. vitamin C, 0.6 mg. beta-carotene • **Serves 4**

Warm
Pleasures

❧ ❧ ❧

FRUIT PASTRIES, WARM SOUFFLÉS,

CRISPS, CRUMBLES AND

OLD-FASHIONED PUDDINGS—

THE SWEET COMFORTS OF HOME

COFFEE CUP SOUFFLÉS

1 tablespoon unsalted butter or margarine, at room temperature

¼ cup plus 1 tablespoon granulated sugar

¼ cup cornstarch

3 tablespoons packed light brown sugar

3 tablespoons unsweetened cocoa powder

1½ teaspoons instant espresso powder

¼ teaspoon ground cinnamon

1¼ cups evaporated skimmed milk

6 large egg whites

⅛ teaspoon salt

2 teaspoons vanilla extract

Espresso beans, for garnish (optional)

What more appropriate servers for a mocha soufflé than coffee cups? They're just the right size, too. Use heavy porcelain cups—don't put your fine bone china in the oven.

1 Preheat the oven to 400°. Coat six 7-ounce ovenproof coffee cups, soufflé dishes or custard cups with the butter or margarine, and dust evenly using 2 tablespoons of the granulated sugar, turning the cups or dishes to coat the sides completely. Place the cups on a baking sheet.

2 In a medium, heavy saucepan, whisk together 2 tablespoons of the remaining granulated sugar, the cornstarch, brown sugar, cocoa powder, espresso powder and cinnamon. Gradually whisk in the evaporated milk until the mixture is smooth.

3 Place the pan over medium heat and cook, whisking frequently and then constantly as the milk mixture gets hotter, until it comes to a boil and thickens. Remove the pan from the heat. Place a sheet of plastic wrap directly onto the surface of the milk mixture to prevent a skin from forming; set aside.

4 In a large bowl, with an electric mixer at high speed, beat the egg whites and salt until foamy. Gradually beat in the remaining 1 tablespoon granulated sugar and continue beating until stiff peaks form.

5 Whisk the vanilla into the milk mixture. Stir a big spoonful of the beaten whites into the milk mixture to lighten it. Then pour the milk mixture into the beaten whites. With a large rubber spatula, fold the milk mixture into the whites until no white streaks remain. Divide the mixture evenly among the prepared cups or dishes.

6 Bake the soufflés for 13 to 15 minutes, or until puffed and firm to the touch. Remove from the oven and serve immediately, garnished with espresso beans, if desired.

Preparation time 10 minutes • **Total time** 45 minutes • **Per serving** 174 calories, 2.4 g. fat (12% of calories), 1.5 g. saturated fat, 7 mg. cholesterol, 166 mg. sodium, 0.8 g. dietary fiber, 168 mg. calcium, 1 mg. iron, 1 mg. vitamin C, 0.2 mg. beta-carotene • **Serves 6**

APPLE-CRANBERRY CRISP

¾ **cup old-fashioned rolled oats or rolled wheat**

⅓ **cup whole-wheat flour**

¼ **cup packed dark brown sugar**

⅛ **teaspoon salt**

⅛ **teaspoon ground allspice**

3 **tablespoons chilled unsalted butter or margarine, cut into small pieces**

3 **large Empire, Idared or Granny Smith apples, cored and sliced into ¼-inch-thick wedges**

½ **cup dried cranberries**

3 **tablespoons frozen apple juice concentrate**

1 **tablespoon granulated sugar**

A basic fruit-crisp topping is made with white flour, but this nicely crunchy version has rolled oats as its main ingredient, along with some whole-wheat flour. Rolled wheat, which is sold in health food stores, may be used in place of the oats. If you can't get dried cranberries, substitute other dried fruits, such as chopped prunes or apricots.

1 Preheat the oven to 425°.

2 In a medium bowl, combine the oats or wheat, flour, brown sugar, salt and allspice. Using your fingers or a pastry blender, lightly mix in the butter or margarine until the mixture is crumbly.

3 In an 8- or 9-inch square baking dish, toss together the apples, cranberries, apple juice concentrate and granulated sugar until well mixed. Sprinkle the oat or wheat mixture evenly over the top.

4 Cover with foil and bake for 20 minutes, or until the mixture is bubbly and the apples are tender. Uncover and bake for 5 to 10 minutes longer, or until the topping is lightly browned.

Preparation time 10 minutes • **Total time** 40 minutes • **Per serving** 188 calories, 5.2 g. fat (25% of calories), 2.8 g. saturated fat, 12 mg. cholesterol, 40 mg. sodium, 3.3 g. dietary fiber, 19 mg. calcium, 1 mg. iron, 10 mg. vitamin C, 0.1 mg. beta-carotene • **Serves 8**

❧   ❧   ❧

The Empire, a tasty cross between a Delicious and a McIntosh, is firmer and crisper than either of its forebears.

The Idared is related to the Jonathan apple. Good for eating fresh, the Idared is also ideal for crisps and pies.

Granny Smith apples are quite hard, but not especially flavorful. Give them an extra pinch of spice and a squeeze of lemon.

Cookies & Bars

❧ ❧ ❧

LEMONY ICEBOX COOKIES, CHEWY
FRUIT BARS, LACY WAFERS, AIRY
MERINGUES—SOMETHING FOR EVERY
COOKIE JAR AND PARTY TABLE

FRUIT AND NUT PINWHEELS

⅔ cup golden raisins

½ cup plus 2 tablespoons raspberry all-fruit preserves

3 tablespoons slivered blanched almonds

1 cup all-purpose flour

¼ cup sugar

2 ounces fat-free cream cheese, softened

2 ounces Neufchâtel cream cheese (⅓ less fat), softened

1 tablespoon plus 1 teaspoon reduced-calorie tub margarine (6 grams of fat per tablespoon)

1 teaspoon ground cinnamon

Old-world pastries like strudel are made by rolling dough around a filling, which can be a tricky task (strudel dough is paper-thin). Making these fruit and nut swirls is simpler, thanks to an easy-to-handle, firm-textured dough that is also low in fat. (Fat-free and Neufchâtel cream cheeses add texture and a rich taste without the fat.) Instead of forming each pinwheel individually, you roll the filling and dough, jelly-roll style, and then slice the roll crosswise.

1 Preheat the oven to 350°. Spray 2 large baking sheets with no-stick spray.

2 In a small bowl, combine the raisins, preserves and almonds; set aside.

3 In a large bowl, with an electric mixer at medium speed, beat the flour, 2 tablespoons of the sugar, the fat-free and Neufchâtel cream cheeses and margarine until well combined. Divide the dough in half and set aside.

4 In another small bowl, combine the remaining 2 tablespoons sugar and the cinnamon. Sprinkle a work surface with half the sugar-cinnamon mixture.

5 Place half the dough on top of the sugar mixture and, with a floured rolling pin, roll out the dough to an 11-inch round. Carefully spread half the raisin-almond mixture over the dough to the edge. Roll up the dough, jelly-roll style, around the filling. Slice the jelly roll into ¼-inch-thick slices, discarding the small end slices, if desired. Arrange the slices on one of the prepared baking sheets; repeat with the remaining sugar mixture, dough and filling.

6 Place both baking sheets in the oven and bake for 12 to 14 minutes (switching the position of the sheets halfway through baking), or until the cookies are golden. Transfer the cookies to wire racks to cool.

Preparation time 10 minutes • **Total time** 45 minutes • **Per cookie** 50 calories, 1 g. fat (19% of calories), 0.3 g. saturated fat, 1 mg. cholesterol, 19 mg. sodium, 0.3 g. dietary fiber, 10 mg. calcium, 0 mg. iron, 0 mg. vitamin C, 0 mg. beta-carotene
Makes 3 dozen cookies

❧ ❧ ❧

GINGER-GINGER COOKIES

2 cups all-purpose flour

1½ teaspoons ground ginger

½ teaspoon baking soda

¼ teaspoon ground allspice

¼ teaspoon ground cinnamon

¼ teaspoon ground cloves

¼ teaspoon salt

¼ cup reduced-calorie tub margarine (8 grams of fat per tablespoon)

½ cup packed dark brown sugar

2 large egg whites

1 teaspoon vanilla extract

1 tablespoon plus 1½ teaspoons minced crystallized ginger (1 ounce)

For round cookies, a drinking glass is a fine alternative to a cookie cutter.

Ginger fans will be pleased to note that their favorite flavor is found in two forms in these rolled-and-cut cookies: There's the usual ground ginger, used as a spice, but the dough is also studded with tantalizing bits of crystallized ginger. With your favorite cookie cutters, match the shape to the holiday or occasion.

1 Spray 2 large baking sheets with no-stick spray; set aside.

2 In a medium bowl, combine the flour, ground ginger, baking soda, allspice, cinnamon, cloves and salt.

3 In a large bowl, with an electric mixer at medium speed, beat the margarine and brown sugar until light and fluffy, about 1 minute. Add the egg whites and vanilla, and beat until well combined.

4 With the mixer at low speed, gradually beat in the dry ingredients until well combined. Stir in the crystallized ginger.

5 Preheat the oven to 400°.

6 On a lightly floured surface, with a floured rolling pin, roll out half the dough to a ¼-inch-thick round. Using cookie cutters in any shapes you prefer, cut out the dough. Arrange the cookies, 1 inch apart, on the prepared baking sheets. Place both baking sheets in the oven and bake the cookies for 5 minutes (switching the position of the sheets halfway through baking), or until the edges of the cookies are lightly browned. Transfer the cookies to wire racks to cool. Repeat with the remaining dough and trimmings.

Preparation time 10 minutes • **Total time** 45 minutes • **Per cookie** 49 calories, 1 g. fat (18% of calories), 0.2 g. saturated fat, 0 mg. cholesterol, 47 mg. sodium, 0.2 g. dietary fiber, 6 mg. calcium, 1 mg. iron, 0 mg. vitamin C, 0 mg. beta-carotene
Makes 3 dozen cookies

KITCHEN TIP
If you dust the work surface and rolling pin too heavily with flour when rolling cookie dough, the cookies will turn out stiff and hard. So dust with a light hand, or use a pastry cloth and stockinette rolling-pin cover, which will keep the dough from sticking.

CHOCOLATE-ORANGE HAZELNUT BISCOTTI

¼ cup shelled hazelnuts

2½ cups all-purpose flour

¼ cup unsweetened cocoa powder

¾ teaspoon baking soda

¼ teaspoon salt

1 cup sugar

2 large eggs

1 large egg white

1½ teaspoons grated orange zest

1 teaspoon vanilla extract

The word *biscotti* means "twice baked," and these Italian specialties do go into the oven twice: The dough, formed into a log, is baked until firm, and then the logs are sliced and rebaked to produce crisp cookies that are traditionally served with a beverage for dunking.

1 Preheat the oven to 350°. Spray a baking sheet with no-stick spray; set aside.

2 Place the hazelnuts in a baking pan and toast for 8 to 10 minutes, or until the skins loosen and the nuts are lightly browned. Place the hazelnuts in a kitchen towel and rub to remove the skins. Finely chop the nuts; set aside. Reduce the oven temperature to 325°.

3 In a large bowl, combine the flour, cocoa powder, baking soda and salt; set aside.

4 In another large bowl, with an electric mixer at medium speed, beat the sugar, eggs, egg white, orange zest and vanilla until well combined. With the mixer at low speed, gradually add the dry ingredients and hazelnuts, and beat until well combined.

5 Turn the dough out onto a lightly floured surface. Shape the dough into two 12-inch-long logs.

6 Place the logs on the prepared baking sheet and bake for 20 to 25 minutes, or until the bottoms are lightly browned and the tops are set. Remove the logs to a wire rack to cool for about 10 minutes, then cut each log diagonally into ½-inch-thick slices. Return the slices to the baking sheet and bake for another 10 to 15 minutes (turning the biscotti once halfway through baking), or until lightly toasted all over. Transfer the biscotti to wire racks to cool completely.

Preparation time 10 minutes • **Total time** 50 minutes • **Per cookie** 59 calories, 0.9 g. fat (13% of calories), 0.2 g. saturated fat, 11 mg. cholesterol, 42 mg. sodium, 0.4 g. dietary fiber, 5 mg. calcium, 1 mg. iron, 0 mg. vitamin C, 0 mg. beta-carotene
Makes 40 cookies

❧ ❧ ❧

Cakes, Pies & Tarts

❧ ❧ ❧

CITRUSY BUNDT CAKE, FROSTED

CHOCOLATE CAKE, PUMPKIN AND

BERRY PIES, LUSCIOUS TARTS—

ALL PREPARED THE HEALTHY WAY

LEMON-LIME CAKE WITH RASPBERRY SAUCE

2 teaspoons all-purpose flour

4 cups cake flour

2½ teaspoons baking powder

½ teaspoon salt

1⅓ cups plain nonfat yogurt

¼ cup fresh lemon juice

¼ cup fresh lime juice

2 teaspoons grated lemon zest

2 teaspoons grated lime zest

2 teaspoons vanilla extract

1½ cups sugar

¼ cup unsalted butter, softened

2 tablespoons canola oil

2 large eggs

2 large egg whites

1 cup Raspberry Sauce, for topping (see recipe page 18)

Although this citrus-suffused cake is far less rich than a standard bundt cake, it is wonderfully moist and keeps well, thanks to the nonfat yogurt in the batter. You don't have to include both lemon and lime: If you prefer, choose one or the other, using a total of ½ cup of juice and 4 teaspoons (1 tablespoon plus 1 teaspoon) of zest.

1 Preheat the oven to 350°. Spray a 10-inch bundt pan with no-stick spray. Dust the pan with the all-purpose flour and tap out any excess.

2 Sift the cake flour, baking powder and salt together into a large bowl; set aside.

3 In a small bowl, stir together the yogurt, lemon juice, lime juice, lemon zest, lime zest and vanilla until well combined; set aside.

4 In another large bowl, with an electric mixer at medium speed, beat the sugar, butter and oil until combined. (It will have a grainy consistency.) Add the whole eggs and egg whites, and beat for about 2 minutes, or until the mixture is smooth and thick. With the mixer at low speed, beat in half the reserved flour mixture and all of the reserved yogurt mixture until well blended. Add the remaining flour mixture and beat until incorporated.

5 Pour the batter into the prepared pan and spread evenly. Bake for 30 to 35 minutes, or until a cake tester inserted into the thickest part of the cake comes out clean. Transfer the pan to a wire rack and let the cake cool in the pan for 10 minutes. Invert the cake and remove from the pan. Transfer to a serving plate to cool completely.

6 When the cake has cooled, cut it into 10 slices and serve with the Raspberry Sauce.

Preparation time 20 minutes • **Total Time** 1 hour plus cooling time • **Per serving with sauce** 416 calories, 10.1 g. fat (24% of calories), 3.5 g. saturated fat, 56 mg. cholesterol, 282 mg. sodium, 1.2 g. dietary fiber, 149 mg. calcium, 4 mg. iron, 12 mg. vitamin C, 0.2 mg. beta-carotene • **Serves 10**

ぺ ぺ ぺ

Preceding pages: Strawberry Meringue Tart (recipe on page 109)

KIWI CUSTARD TART

Tart Shell

- 1 cup all-purpose flour
- 1 teaspoon sugar
- ½ teaspoon lemon zest
- ¼ teaspoon salt
- 2 tablespoons chilled unsalted butter, cut into small pieces
- 2 tablespoons canola oil
- 3 tablespoons nonfat sour cream
- 2 to 2½ teaspoons cold water

Custard

- 1¼ cups 1% low-fat milk
- 1 vanilla bean, split
- One 3-inch-long piece lemon zest
- ¼ cup sugar
- 2 tablespoons cornstarch
- Pinch of salt
- 1 large egg plus 1 large egg white, lightly beaten

Fruit Topping

- 5 kiwifruits, peeled and sliced ¼ inch thick (see pages 14–15 for peeling instructions)

B ake this gorgeous fruit-topped tart when you really want to impress someone. Keep an eye on the tart shell while it's baking; if the edge browns too quickly, cover it with strips of foil.

1 For the tart shell, in a food processor, combine the flour, sugar, lemon zest and salt, and pulse to mix. Add the butter and oil, and pulse until the mixture resembles coarse meal. Add the sour cream and 2 teaspoons of the water, and process until the dough comes together. (Add a few drops of water if the dough seems dry.) Flatten the dough into a disk, wrap in plastic wrap and refrigerate for 15 minutes.

2 Meanwhile, start the custard: In a small saucepan, bring the milk, vanilla bean and lemon zest to a simmer over medium-high heat. Remove the pan from the heat, cover and let the mixture steep while the dough chills.

3 Preheat the oven to 400°. On a lightly floured surface, roll out the dough to a 10-inch round about ⅛ inch thick. Place the dough in a 9-inch tart pan and gently press it into the bottom and sides of the pan. Trim the edges and prick the bottom with a fork. Place the pan in the freezer for 5 minutes, then line the tart shell with foil and fill it with pie weights. Bake the tart shell for 8 to 10 minutes, remove the weights and foil, and bake for another 5 minutes. Transfer to a rack to cool.

4 Meanwhile, for the custard, in a medium bowl, combine the sugar, cornstarch and salt. Add the beaten egg and egg white, and beat well with a wooden spoon. Remove the lemon zest from the reserved milk mixture and scrape the seeds from the vanilla bean into the milk. Slowly add the warm milk to the egg mixture, stirring constantly until well combined. Pour the custard into the cooled tart shell and bake for 15 minutes. Transter to a wire rack to cool briefly.

5 For the topping, arrange the kiwifruit on top of the custard, starting from the outside edge. Serve the tart at room temperature.

Preparation time 15 minutes • **Total Time** 1 hour • **Per serving** 209 calories, 7.6 g. fat (33% of calories), 2.5 g. saturated fat, 36 mg. cholesterol, 125 mg. sodium, 2 g. dietary fiber, 74 mg. calcium, 1 mg. iron, 37 mg. vitamin C, 0.2 mg. beta-carotene
Serves 8

SPICED CARROT CAKE

Cake

2 cups finely shredded carrots

¼ cup fresh lemon juice

1 cup all-purpose flour

1 cup whole-wheat flour

2 teaspoons ground cinnamon

1 teaspoon baking soda

½ teaspoon baking powder

½ teaspoon ground ginger

½ teaspoon salt

¼ teaspoon ground cloves

¼ teaspoon ground nutmeg

⅛ teaspoon freshly ground black pepper

⅔ cup honey

⅓ cup plain nonfat yogurt

¼ cup canola or safflower oil

1 large egg

1 cup golden raisins

Topping

1 tablespoon confectioners' sugar

¼ teaspoon ground cinnamon

¼ teaspoon ground ginger

Carrot cake has an undeserved reputation as some sort of "health food," simply because it has carrots in it. But along with those carrots you usually get (at least) a cup of oil and 4 eggs—not to mention a half-pound of cream cheese and a stick of butter for the frosting. You'll find this delightfully spiced single-layer cake a refreshing change from the old-fashioned version. For an exceptionally pretty cake, dust the confectioners' sugar through a lacy doily, or place small paper cutouts (geometric shapes, hearts, stars or whatever you like) on top of the cake before sifting the sugar over it.

1 Preheat the oven to 350°. Spray a 9-inch round cake pan with no-stick spray. Line the bottom with a circle of wax paper and spray again.

2 For the cake, in a large bowl, combine the carrots and lemon juice.

3 In a medium bowl, combine the all-purpose flour, whole-wheat flour, cinnamon, baking soda, baking powder, ginger, salt, cloves, nutmeg and black pepper, and whisk until well blended.

4 In a small bowl, combine the honey, yogurt, oil and egg.

5 Add the honey mixture to the carrot mixture and stir well. Add the flour mixture and the raisins, and stir until well combined.

6 Pour the batter into the prepared cake pan and spread evenly. Bake for 40 to 45 minutes, or until a cake tester inserted in the center of the cake comes out clean. Transfer the pan to a wire rack and let the cake cool for 10 minutes. When cooled, transfer the cake to a serving plate.

7 For the topping, in a small bowl, combine the confectioners' sugar, cinnamon and ginger. Place the sugar mixture in a small strainer and sprinkle over the top of the cake (in a pattern, if desired).

Preparation time 15 minutes • **Total Time** 1 hour plus cooling time • **Per serving** 276 calories, 6.5 g. fat (21% of calories), 0.6 g. saturated fat, 21 mg. cholesterol, 283 mg. sodium, 3.3 g. dietary fiber, 60 mg. calcium, 2 mg. iron, 6 mg. vitamin C, 3.7 mg. beta-carotene • **Serves 10**

STRAWBERRY MERINGUE TART

¼ **cup cornstarch, sifted**

¼ **cup finely ground blanched almonds**

¾ **cup sugar**

3 **large egg whites, at room temperature**

⅛ **teaspoon cream of tartar**

Pinch of salt

1 **teaspoon vanilla extract**

1½ **pints strawberries, hulled and left whole**

2 **tablespoons seedless raspberry all-fruit preserves**

2 **teaspoons water**

Mint sprigs, for garnish (optional)

To make a simple shell, first spread some of the meringue into a flat round, then spoon dollops of the remaining meringue around the edges.

This elegant confection has a meringue shell rather than a pastry crust. The chewy meringue bakes more quickly, and in a hotter oven, than traditional meringues, emerging a delicate tan rather than a pure white.

1 Preheat the oven to 300°. Line a baking sheet with foil and lightly spray with no-stick spray.

2 In a small bowl, combine the cornstarch, almonds and ¼ cup of the sugar; set aside.

3 In a large bowl, with an electric mixer at medium speed, beat the egg whites, cream of tartar and salt until soft peaks form. With the mixer at medium-high speed, slowly add the remaining ½ cup sugar, 1 tablespoon at a time, continuing to beat until the egg whites are stiff but not dry. With the mixer at high speed, beat in the vanilla. Gently fold in the almond mixture.

4 Using a large spoon, or a pastry bag without a tip, spread enough of the meringue on the baking sheet to form an 8- or 9-inch round about ¾-inch thick. With the spoon, drop spoonfuls of the remaining meringue around the edge to form a border about 1 inch high. Or, use a pastry bag fitted with a large rosette tip to pipe a fancier border.

5 Bake the meringue shell on the bottom rack of the oven for 30 minutes, or until light tan and crisp. Transfer the baking sheet to a wire rack and let the meringue cool on the baking sheet for 5 minutes. Carefully peel off the foil, then transfer the meringue shell to a serving plate. Fill the shell with the strawberries.

6 In a small saucepan, combine the preserves and water, and melt over low heat. Strain into a small bowl. Using a pastry brush, lightly glaze the strawberries with the melted preserves. Serve the tart at room temperature, garnished with mint sprigs, if desired.

Preparation time 20 minutes • **Total time** 1 hour 10 minutes • **Per serving** 143 calories, 1.9 g. fat (12% of calories), 0.2 g. saturated fat, 0 mg. cholesterol, 39 mg. sodium, 1.9 g. dietary fiber, 17 mg. calcium, 0 mg. iron, 34 mg. vitamin C, 0 mg. beta-carotene • **Serves 8**

❧ ❧ ❧

DEVIL'S FOOD CAKE WITH RASPBERRIES

Cake

1 cup unsweetened cocoa powder

2 cups cake flour

¾ cup packed light brown sugar

½ cup granulated sugar

1½ teaspoons baking powder

½ teaspoon baking soda

½ teaspoon salt

1 cup strong black decaffeinated coffee

1 cup low-fat buttermilk

2 large egg whites, at room temperature

¼ cup canola or safflower oil

1 teaspoon vanilla extract

Frosting

1½ cups granulated sugar

¼ cup water

1 tablespoon light corn syrup

2 large egg whites

¼ teaspoon salt

1 teaspoon vanilla extract

2 squares (2 ounces) unsweetened chocolate, melted

Topping

½ pint fresh raspberries

1 tablespoon confectioners' sugar

The icing for this chocolate cake should be made just before you plan to use it, or it may become too stiff to spread. If need be, warm it in a microwave for a few seconds to soften it.

1 Preheat the oven to 325°. Lightly spray two 8-inch round cake pans with no-stick spray. Lightly dust the pans with a small amount of the cocoa powder, tapping out the excess.

2 For the cake, in a large bowl, combine the remaining cocoa, the flour, brown sugar, granulated sugar, baking powder, baking soda and salt. In another large bowl, with an electric mixer at medium speed, beat the coffee, buttermilk, egg whites, oil and vanilla. With the mixer at low speed, add the cocoa mixture and beat until just combined. Divide the batter between the prepared pans and bake for 30 minutes, or until a tester inserted in each comes out clean. Transfer the pans to wire racks to cool for 10 minutes before turning the cakes out.

3 Make the frosting just before you plan to use it. In a medium saucepan, combine the sugar, water and corn syrup. Bring to a simmer over medium-high heat, then cover and simmer for 2 minutes. Uncover and simmer for 2 more minutes, or until the syrup reaches 245° on a candy thermometer. Remove the pan from the heat.

4 In a large bowl, with an electric mixer at medium speed, beat the egg whites with the salt for 1 to 2 minutes, or until soft peaks form. While you beat the egg whites, return the syrup mixture just to a boil. With the mixer at medium-high, pour the hot syrup into the egg whites, immediately increase the mixer speed to high and continue to beat until the mixture is stiff and glossy. Beat in the vanilla, then stir in the melted chocolate until the mixture is smooth.

5 Transfer one cake layer to a plate and frost with ½ cup of the frosting. Place the other layer on top and frost the rest of the cake. Arrange the raspberries on top of the cake. Dust with the confectioners' sugar.

Preparation time 15 minutes • **Total time** 1 hour plus cooling time • **Per serving** 360 calories, 8.8 g. fat (22% of calories), 2.7 g. saturated fat, 1 mg. cholesterol, 289 mg. sodium, 3.3 g. dietary fiber, 90 mg. calcium, 3 mg. iron, 3 mg. vitamin C, 0 mg. beta-carotene • **Serves 12**

ANGEL CAKE WITH CHOCOLATE SAUCE

Cake

1 **cup cake flour, sifted 3 times**

1½ **cups sugar**

12 **large egg whites, at room temperature**

1 **tablespoon orange-flower water**

½ **teaspoon vanilla extract**

½ **teaspoon cream of tartar**

¼ **teaspoon salt**

1 **tablespoon grated orange zest**

Chocolate Sauce

¼ **cup plus 1 tablespoon sugar**

¼ **cup fresh orange juice**

¼ **cup water**

½ **cup unsweetened cocoa powder**

Topping (optional)

Orange slices

Fragrant with citrus, this cloud-light cake is flavored with orange zest and also with orange-flower water, which is made from orange blossoms. You can buy it at many liquor stores, at pharmacies and at Indian or Near Eastern grocery stores.

1 Preheat the oven to 350°.

2 For the cake, in a small bowl, whisk together the cake flour and ½ cup of the sugar; set aside.

3 In a large bowl, with an electric mixer at medium speed, beat the egg whites, orange-flower water, vanilla, cream of tartar and salt until soft peaks form. With the mixer at medium-high speed, slowly add the remaining 1 cup sugar, a tablespoon at a time, continuing to beat until the whites are stiff but not dry. Gently fold the reserved flour-sugar mixture into the egg whites, then fold in the orange zest.

4 Pour the batter into a 10-inch tube pan and run a knife through the batter to remove any air bubbles. Bake for 30 minutes, or until the top springs back when lightly touched and a cake tester or toothpick inserted in the center comes out clean.

5 Remove the cake from the oven and invert on a wire rack. Let cool in this position until the pan is no longer hot. To remove the cake, run a sharp, thin-bladed knife around the sides and inner tube of the pan. Lift the cake out of the pan then remove the bottom of the pan. Place the cake on a serving plate.

6 For the sauce, in small saucepan, combine the sugar, orange juice and water, and bring to a boil over medium-high heat. Reduce the heat to low and whisk in the cocoa powder until smooth.

7 If desired, top the whole cake with orange slices before cutting. Serve with the chocolate sauce.

Preparation time 15 minutes • **Total time** 55 minutes plus cooling time • **Per serving** 268 calories, 0.8 g. fat (3% of calories), 0.4 g. saturated fat, 0 mg. cholesterol, 152 mg. sodium, 1.6 g. dietary fiber, 15 mg. calcium, 2 mg. iron, 4 mg. vitamin C, 0 mg. beta-carotene • **Serves 8**

Zucchini Cake with Lemon Syrup

Cake

1½ cups cake flour

1 teaspoon baking soda

1 teaspoon ground cinnamon

½ teaspoon Chinese five-spice powder (optional)

¼ teaspoon salt

1½ cups firmly packed finely shredded zucchini

⅔ cup firmly packed light brown sugar

⅓ cup canola oil

½ cup golden raisins or dried cranberries

2 large egg whites

Lemon Syrup

½ cup granulated sugar

¼ cup water

3 tablespoons fresh lemon juice

You can use the shredding disk of your food processor to grate the zucchini quickly.

Cinnamon is a requisite for spicy cakes and cookies, but you've probably never tasted a dessert made with Chinese five-spice powder, a heady blend of cinnamon, anise, cloves, Szechuan peppercorns and, sometimes, cardamom. If you can't get this ingredient, try adding a pinch each of ground cloves and ground cardamom along with the cinnamon.

1 Preheat the oven to 350°. Spray an 8½ x 4½-inch loaf pan with no-stick spray.

2 For the cake, in a small bowl, combine the flour, baking soda, cinnamon, five-spice powder, if using, and salt; set aside.

3 In a medium bowl, combine the zucchini, sugar, oil and raisins or cranberries. Add the flour mixture and stir to combine. Set aside.

4 In a large bowl, with an electric mixer at medium speed, beat the egg whites until frothy. With the mixer at medium-high speed, beat until the whites stiffen. Gently fold the egg whites into the zucchini mixture.

5 Spoon the batter into the prepared pan, spread evenly and bake for 40 to 45 minutes, or until a cake tester inserted in the center of the cake comes out clean. Transfer the pan to a wire rack and allow the cake to cool in the pan for 10 minutes.

6 While the cake is cooling, make the syrup. In a small saucepan, combine the sugar and water, and bring to a boil over medium-high heat. Let the mixture boil for 8 to 10 minutes, or until it is a golden-amber color. Remove the pan from the heat and stir in the lemon juice.

7 Remove the cake from the pan and cut it into 10 slices. Serve each slice with some of the lemon syrup.

Preparation time 10 minutes • **Total time** 1 hour 5 minutes • **Per serving** 249 calories, 7.5 g. fat (27% of calories), 0.6 g. saturated fat, 0 mg. cholesterol, 200 mg. sodium, 0.6 g. dietary fiber, 28 mg. calcium, 2 mg. iron, 5 mg. vitamin C, 0.1 mg. beta-carotene • **Serves 10**

FOUR-BERRY PIE

Crust

> 2 cups all-purpose flour
>
> 2 teaspoons sugar
>
> ½ teaspoon salt
>
> 4 tablespoons chilled unsalted butter, cut into small pieces
>
> 4 tablespoons canola oil
>
> 6 tablespoons nonfat sour cream
>
> 1 tablespoon cold water, plus 1 additional teaspoon, if necessary
>
> ¼ teaspoon almond extract

Filling

> 2 cups halved fresh strawberries
>
> 2 cups fresh raspberries
>
> 1 cup fresh blackberries
>
> 1 cup fresh blueberries
>
> 3 tablespoons fresh lemon juice
>
> ¾ cup to 1 cup sugar, depending on sweetness of fruit
>
> 3 tablespoons cornstarch
>
> 3 tablespoons instant tapioca
>
> 1 tablespoon sugar, for topping (optional)

Here's ample incentive for a trip to a "pick-your-own" berry farm. The crisscross lattice topping is a simplified version of the traditional under-and-over weaving method.

1 For the crust, in a food processor, combine the flour, sugar and salt, and pulse briefly to mix. Add the butter and oil, and pulse until the mixture resembles coarse meal. Add the sour cream, 1 tablespoon of the cold water and the almond extract, and process until the mixture just comes together. (If the dough seems too dry, add a few more drops of cold water.) Gather the dough and shape it into two disks; wrap in plastic wrap and refrigerate for at least 15 minutes, or until ready to use. The dough can be refrigerated for up to a day.

2 Meanwhile, make the filling: In a large bowl, combine the fruit and lemon juice. In a small bowl, combine the sugar, cornstarch and tapioca. Stir the sugar mixture into the fruit; let sit for 15 minutes.

3 Preheat the oven to 400°. Adjust the oven rack to the bottom shelf. Line a baking sheet with foil.

4 While the oven is heating, on a well-floured surface, roll out the dough to two 10-inch rounds about ⅛ inch thick. Keeping one round covered, fit the other round into a 9- or 10-inch pie plate, leaving the overhang. Spoon the filling into the shell. Cut the remaining round into ¾-inch-wide strips. Place half the strips over the filling at a 45° angle, spacing them evenly. Place the remaining strips at an opposing angle to the first strips to form a lattice pattern. Trim the ends of the lattice strips and the bottom crust to a ½-inch overhang, then fold the bottom crust over the lattice ends and crimp or pinch the edge to seal.

5 Place the pie on the prepared baking sheet and bake for 45 to 50 minutes, or until the crust is golden brown and the juices begin to bubble. Transfer the pie to a wire rack and let cool for 15 minutes before serving.

Preparation time 10 minutes • **Total time** 1 hour 20 minutes plus cooling time
Per serving 394 calories, 13.3 g. fat (30% of calories), 4.1 g. saturated fat, 16 mg. cholesterol, 165 mg. sodium, 4.5 g. dietary fiber, 41 mg. calcium, 2 mg. iron, 38 mg. vitamin C, 0.2 mg. beta-carotene • **Serves 8**

❧ ❧ ❧

ZUCCOTTO

1 container (32 ounces) vanilla
low-fat yogurt

¼ cup blanched slivered almonds

One (13.6-ounce) fat-free
pound cake

3 tablespoons fresh orange juice

2 tablespoons sweet Marsala wine

½ cup confectioners' sugar

1 square (1 ounce) semisweet
chocolate, finely chopped

1 envelope unflavored gelatin

¼ cup cold water

Sliced strawberries, for topping
(optional)

Arrange enough pieces of cake in the bowl
so they line it snugly. This layer of cake
will form the dome that holds the filling.

In Italian, *zuccotto* means "skullcap"; this impressive dessert was apparently named for its domed shape. Substitute orange juice for the Marsala if you prefer to omit the alcohol.

1 Line a strainer with a double layer of paper towels and place over a medium bowl. Spoon in the yogurt and let drain for 4 hours. Discard the whey and spoon the yogurt into the bowl; refrigerate until needed.

2 Preheat the oven to 350°. Place the almonds in a baking pan and toast for about 8 minutes, or until lightly browned. Chop the nuts.

3 Spray a deep 8-cup bowl with no-stick spray. Line the bowl with plastic wrap. Cut the pound cake into twenty ¼-inch-thick slices. Place one whole slice of cake in the center of the bottom of the bowl. Cut the remaining slices in half diagonally. Arrange enough cake triangles around the inside of the bowl to cover the bowl, overlapping to fit.

4 In a cup, combine the orange juice and Marsala. Brush the cake slices with some of the orange juice mixture; set the remainder aside.

5 Add the confectioners' sugar, chocolate and toasted almonds to the drained yogurt, stirring until well combined. In a small saucepan, sprinkle the gelatin over the cold water and let stand for 1 minute. Cook over low heat, stirring, for 2 to 3 minutes, or until the gelatin dissolves. Gradually whisk the gelatin mixture into the yogurt mixture, whisking constantly until it is completely incorporated.

6 Gently spoon the yogurt mixture into the bowl to cover the cake. Cover the yogurt mixture completely with the remaining cake slices. Brush the remaining orange juice mixture onto the cake slices. Cover with plastic wrap and chill for at least 3 hours, or overnight.

7 To serve, uncover and invert the zuccotto onto a platter. Remove the bowl and plastic wrap. Top with sliced strawberries, if desired.

Preparation time 5 minutes • **Total time** 35 minutes plus draining and chilling time
Per serving 183 calories, 3.4 g. fat (17% of calories), 0.6 g. saturated fat, 2 mg. cholesterol, 137 mg. sodium, 0.8 g. dietary fiber, 89 mg. calcium, 0 mg. iron, 2 mg. vitamin C, 0.1 mg. beta-carotene • **Serves 12**

PUMPKIN PIE

Crust

1½ cups graham cracker crumbs

1 tablespoon margarine, softened

1 tablespoon canola oil

1 teaspoon ground ginger

1 teaspoon grated orange zest

1 tablespoon light corn syrup

1 tablespoon cold water, plus
   1 teaspoon, if necessary

Filling

2 large egg whites

1 large egg

¾ cup firmly packed dark brown
   sugar

1 teaspoon ground cinnamon

½ teaspoon ground ginger

½ teaspoon ground nutmeg

¼ teaspoon mace

¼ teaspoon salt

2 cups solid-pack canned
   pumpkin

1 can (12 ounces) evaporated
   skimmed milk

1 teaspoon vanilla extract

Topping

½ cup nonfat sour cream

1 tablespoon confectioners' sugar

1 teaspoon vanilla extract or
   ½ vanilla bean, split and scraped

Ground nutmeg, for garnish
(optional)

What a dream come true: a pumpkin pie light enough to allow for guilt-free "seconds!" Even the creamy topping is low in fat (but the pie is delicious without it, too).

1 Preheat the oven to 400°. Spray a 9-inch pie plate with no-stick spray.

2 For the crust, in a food processor, combine the graham cracker crumbs, margarine, oil, ginger and orange zest, and pulse briefly.

3 In a cup, combine the corn syrup and cold water. Add it to the crumb mixture and process until the mixture begins to hold together. (If the mixture appears dry, add a few more drops of water.) Press the crumb mixture onto the bottom and sides of the prepared pie plate. Bake for about 8 minutes, or until the crust is firm to the touch. Transfer the pie plate to a wire rack and let the crust cool briefly.

4 Meanwhile, make the filling: In a small bowl, lightly beat the egg whites and egg; set aside. In a food processor, combine the brown sugar, cinnamon, ginger, nutmeg, mace and salt, and pulse until well combined. Add the pumpkin, evaporated milk, reserved eggs and vanilla. Pulse just until combined, then process just until smooth.

5 Pour the filling into the prepared pie shell and bake on the middle oven rack for 35 minutes, or until the crust is browned and the filling is just set in the center. Transfer the pie to a rack to cool completely at room temperature or chill in the refrigerator until ready to serve.

6 While the pie is baking, make the topping: In a small bowl, combine the sour cream, confectioners' sugar and vanilla extract or vanilla bean; cover and refrigerate until ready to use.

7 To serve, cut the pie into 8 slices and top each slice with some of the sour cream mixture. Sprinkle with a little nutmeg, if desired.

Preparation time 15 minutes • **Total time** 50 minutes • **Per serving** 296 calories, 5.7 g. fat (17% of calories), 0.7 g. saturated fat, 29 mg. cholesterol, 320 mg. sodium, 1.8 g. dietary fiber, 200 mg. calcium, 2 mg. iron, 4 mg. vitamin C, 8.3 mg. beta-carotene • **Serves 8**

INDEX

❧ ❧ ❧